EXPRESSIONS FROM
THE HEART

Edited by

Simon Harwin

First published in Great Britain in 2003 by
POETRY NOW
Remus House,
Coltsfoot Drive,
Peterborough, PE2 9JX
Telephone (01733) 898101
Fax (01733) 313524

HB ISBN 1 84460 960 X
SB ISBN 1 84460 961 8

FOREWORD

Although we are a nation of poets we are accused of not reading poetry, or buying poetry books. After many years of listening to the incessant gripes of poetry publishers, I can only assume that the books they publish, in general, are books that most people do not want to read.

Poetry should not be obscure, introverted, and as cryptic as a crossword puzzle: it is the poet's duty to reach out and embrace the world.

The world owes the poet nothing and we should not be expected to dig and delve into a rambling discourse searching for some inner meaning.

The reason we write poetry (and almost all of us do) is because we want to communicate: an ideal; an idea; or a specific feeling. Poetry is as essential in communication, as a letter; a radio; a telephone, and the main criterion for selecting the poems in this anthology is very simple: they communicate.

CONTENTS

RENEWED DELIGHTS

His lack of knowledge, when a child,
Recalls him learning now, near end of life,
The ocean ignorance he glimpsed
That made him child again. For now
Upwelling joy returns when sun
Ignites a sky at dawn or spread
Of bluebells in a wood delights
His eye. Too long his mind has ruled
His feelings held in chains. Too long
His focused search for truths had starved
His soul of other means of grace.
But now his mellowed thoughts allow
A sense of awe to reign anew,
As grandchild finds her world is filled
With savoured instances of bliss.

Henry Disney

A MOTHER'S WISH

Listen to the trees, my love,
For they sing so sweetly.
Keep your eyes fixed on the ocean,
For it runs so deeply.
Watch the mighty eagle,
For he moves so swiftly.
Cherish every sunrise
That nature kindly lends thee.
Your voice is now my song, my love,
That fills my soul with such emotion
And blessed love so strong and pure,
Runs deeper than the ocean.
Time passes, as the eagle,
So swiftly flying by,
Yet within the essence of your beauty,
Eternity I find,
For each sunrise that you give me,
Within your loving eyes,
I'll hold with me forever
And cherish every smile,
For God has kindly lent me
An angel from above,
May your life be filled with sunshine
And each moment filled with love.

S Russel

TO SOMEONE VERY SPECIAL

When she smiles, it's like a magical sunrise,
Full cherry lips and eyes that sparkle.
How can I resist the warm wind of her emotion, I surmise,
Alas she is with another and I am heartbroken.
How can I break the spell? I wish to yell.

Love is a dangerous word to utter
As a flower of intense beauty, too much over-zealous attention it dies,
So if interest is carelessly challenged will friendship disappear or wilt.
Or will it blossom into a bucket of colour and perfume sweet?
Am I just in a wonderful dream daze where realism is unwanted in
my blinked gaze?

Is desire not fuelled by envy and passion tinged with tangled jealousy?
A dizzy nomad am I, drifting through the spectre of life, a half,
Searching an anchor of image etched on other's faces, a wanting
to be wanted.
My mirror is cracked and distorted with ugly refrain but look deeper,
deeper without disdain,
Not monster but warm, loving, passionate a knight obscured by
mask and locked in a box
Labelled misfit, pity is not my trophy, but love of equal parallel.

Your lively eye in our banter pierces deep in my defences without care,
We laugh, walk, embrace and onlookers stare, but you demand
no shame.
What can I do caught in your spell? I'm damned unless we grow
in harmony.
What now?

Iain Speed

002

What beauty have I not seen
In wonder, life or dream

That can compare with
A face so fair,
Lips so soft,
Eyes so deep?

Oh, what other beauty could
Compare with a face so fair?

Daniel Lumb

CHRISTMAS PAST

For when we went carolling
We knew just where to go
We knew we were expected
We'd get a warm hello
But unlike it is today
We'd know all the words
Else to go carol-singing
Would really be absurd
Because it was street theatre
Each household would applaud
And give a glass of sherry
To warm the vocal chords
For when we went carolling
Out there in all that snow
There was a festive spirit
Christmases long ago.

John Smurthwaite

LOVE LIFE

Years ago, I admitted it.
Months ago, I shared.
Weeks ago, I regretted it.
Days ago, I'm scared.

Hours ago, I met you.
Minutes ago, I held.
Seconds ago, I fell in love.
Now, you are my world.

Stephen Howsam

TIMES PAST

Green hills of Somerset . . .
Green fields of home -
In memory, I wander,
Content . . . and alone,
To pause beside the sunlit brook
And listen to its song;
Where wild flowers spring
From every nook
And birds sing all day long;
To stand knee-deep in summer grass
With daisies round my feet,
Watching the darting dragonflies
Flash past - in the noonday heat . . .
To climb again, the fern-clad hill
Where foxgloves bend in the breeze
And listen to the music
In the dainty Silver Birch trees;
To gaze across the valley
As the sun is sinking low
To the purple hills in the distance . . .
My dreaming village, far below;
To tread again the well-known path,
As I did in days of yore
And see, in the dusk, the lights of home
Streaming through the open door.
All vanished, now, in the mists of Time,
But whilst memory remains,
I can walk again the green hills of home,
Fragrant meadows . . . and leafy lanes.

Elizabeth Amy Johns

JUST A MEMORY

When the harbour's surrounded
By its myriad of lights
And ships stand silhouetted
'Neath a moon shining bright.
When the wind howls no longer,
Clouds so gently sail by,
Forming shapes quite fantastic
In a vast, boundless sky.
When the water laps gently,
All is calm and serene,
I will stand and recapture
What seems now like a dream.

It is moments like that, which
Make one's life worthwhile,
For my heart filled with pleasure,
On my lips was a smile.
Whilst you stood there beside me
Of my thoughts unaware,
I asked God to watch o'er you
With His own loving care.
And where'er you may travel,
On the land or the sea,
May the 'good' things life holds
Be forever with thee.

Esther Hawkins

FOREVER

As I hold you beneath the stars
The moonlight upon your hair
I am at one with the universe
You must know how much I care

The tender glow, deep in your eyes
Makes the Venus star to wane
Unrivalled in the galaxies
An angel, on earthly plane

When you are near, the cosmos fades
The planets fall from the sky
Nothing exists except we two
Though I know not how or why

Strange powers shatter the fabric of space
The time web for you and for me
Alone my love, I will hold you close
Through all eternity.

John Nolan

A MOMENT IN TIME

Could this be true, that I'm lying beside you?
Watching you as you sleep.
Could this be true that my heart swells?
My passions awaken
As I gently stroke your face, touch your hair.
Could this be me?
As I stand before myself
For the first time a woman and I feel
Vulnerable, wide open,
Yet strangely centred,
As I wholly give myself to this almost unbelieving
Feeling of love I have for you.
Is this me breathing, drinking in the scent of your nakedness?
As I curl my body around yours and kiss the nape of your neck,
Is . . . is this me?
Full of desire,
Letting the desire take me over, ripples of pleasure sweeping up
                                                      and over my body,
As my hands wander and linger around the contours of your body.
Yes this is me, caught up in this moment in time.

Lisa May Matthews

BIRTHRIGHT

As the first blush of dawn
brushes the horizon
I think of you;
At each choral surprise
that opens our eyes
I think of you;
Like sun-kissed clouds
come noon, my lips
find yours;
Our lives, our own
to have, to hold
for all time;
Sharing every moment's
passing, Heaven
surpassing;
Earth, no gentle mother
to us but extending
her blessing . . .
to lovers everywhere
no matter colour,
creed, sex;
Nor sexuality missing out,
fingers pointing put
to rout;
Sun, moon and stars
but reflections
in our eyes;
As for me, no fairer dawn
than the day you
were born.

R N Taber

SPECIAL DAY
(Dedicated to my wife, Caroline Miller)

From the moment you told me
I feel there is a hole in my life,
Knowing you no longer wish to be my wife.

Everything I ever wished for has now been
Taken away, all I have to live for now
Is to get you back some day.

I know in your heart you'll love me,
Like you did that day, when you said, 'I will,'
On our special day, my feelings will never
Change for you, they will always be the same.

It hurts so bad knowing that I'm not the one
You want anymore, no one will ever make me feel the way you did
On our special day, now I wait to hold you again
Deep within my arms.

Love Gary.

Gary Miller

MY SPECIAL PLACE

There's a special place I like to go -
It's very far away,
A place where no one knows my name
And night-time lasts all day.
It's a place where people look at me
And see what's deep inside,
They see someone who laughs and smiles
And bleeds and hurts and cries.
It's a place where no one tells me what
To do or how to be,
A place where I can please myself and
Live my life for me.
And in this place I have a special friend
Who's always there,
Someone to talk to when I'm lonely
And hold me when I'm scared.
This person never hurts, takes offence
Or runs away,
My friend just loves me more and more
And we grow stronger every day.
There's a special place I like to go,
A place that's mine to keep,
The only way to get there, I close my eyes
And go to sleep.

Neil J Oldham

UNTITLED

Do you remember when you fell in love
The moment you decided that your life was incomplete
The day you knew that things could never be the same
Without the one that made your pulse race and your heart beat?

Hold onto the promises you've made today
Try not to let them fade like the wishes and the flowers
When the icing on the cake has all gone soft
And the photographs lie dusty in the loft.

It's true that people change as they grow older
Grow together, respect the other's point of view
Don't lose sight of what you like about each other
The grass is never greener - it's just new.

Loving someone isn't always easy
Sometimes life can leave us all a little frayed
Build a life together, based on love and laughter
And when you stand back - you'll be proud of what you've made.

May the warmth and affection of your friends and family
Cover you like a warm blanket
And the happiness and love you share today
Last a lifetime.

Paula Hickford

TOGETHER

Your love for each other
Has brought you here today
A wish to spend eternity together

To share with each other
Your dreams, wishes and hopes
To laugh, cry and be joyous together

To find strength in each other
United in battle against
The rough times to be fought together

To mould with each other
And nurture an understanding
Of individuality and respect together

To agree to be with each other
Faithful, honest and true
As you both grow in love and life together

To spend with each other
A long and lasting friendship
And may there be peace in your marriage together.

Jackie Kirk

WELCOME

Welcome little one
It is hard to describe
How wonderful it feels
To have you in our lives
You are going to be cherished
Wrapped in undying love
Swaddled in devotion
You are our gift from above
We will guide you always
Watching with care
As you learn new things
When in wonder you stare
You will have the best
That we can give you
We will gently mould
This wonderful life new
With each step you take
Along life's way
You will have our hearts and souls
Each and every day.

Audrey Evans

MY TIME IN WOTTON LAWN

When I was ill and so desperate
I tried so hard to do my best
because in God I began to look
sometimes I felt I could scream.

But then I heard a voice say, 'Just believe and pray
because I am with you all the time and every day.'
He seemed to be with me all the time
even in my song and nursery rhyme.

Then into hospital I did go
it was Wotton Lawn you know
when I got there I did feel
so unloved and so unreal.

Then little by little there seemed to be
lots and lots of friends for me
there came Julia and Christine
we really seemed to be a team.

Then came along a girl called Joan
who said she felt so all alone
I could not believe my ears
because in her life and in her time
her story was so much like mine.

Every morning, just at nine
it was tea and coffee time.
We went to the Royal Hospital and shop
to spend our money till we dropped.

The doctor came and said, 'Don't moan,
next weekend you are going home.'
I cleaned the house and watched TV
It seemed a real treat to me.

Sandra Pitt

THE RAG AND BONE MAN USED TO COME

Every Thursday.
He would blow his trumpet,
an old battered brass one.

He didn't make music,
just arbitrary sounds.
It was all
I needed.

I would chase
him around the
streets.

Sometimes he had
a van; other times
he had his horse:
a great
ugly,
tired
brute
of a horse.

This was no place
for horse s***,
I would think.

To be honest
I was a bit
frightened
of the thing.

I gave him
bin bags full
of things.

One time
I even gave him
my sister's
Communion dress.
(Which had to be quickly retrieved)

All I got in return
was a balloon.

But, to see a balloon
dance in the air
was much better
than any
music.

Brian Conaghan

CREATION

He lies in my arms,
This child we have created.
Brought into existence
With love and tenderness.
Yesterday, he had slept
In my body,
Warmly wrapped in dreams
Of his tomorrow.
A soul apart.
Then he arrived,
Rushing out at me,
His new lungs proving to my ears
Their health and strength.
Reprimanding me for being slow
And tired with labour
Whilst he was all impatience
To begin his life.
My little one.

Flesh of my flesh,
Made by us as proof that we
Should live upon this Earth
In spirit,
Long after we had left
To walk the wind together.

I kissed his wrinkled brow
And saw my face, his father's face
In the perfect features.
We lay together.
Close, bonded at last.
We slept.

Margaret Walker

FROM A NEW GRANDPARENT

So clever they are, the young ones today,
They don't need their God, they don't need to pray,
With their brash self-assurance bright in their eyes
They're still at a loss when the baby cries.

Top marks at school and a first class degree,
Computers, the newest technology,
They know all the facts, but what a surprise -
They're just helpless kids when the baby cries!

The latest gadgets that money can buy
Won't make him sleep and they're wondering why,
But love, trial and error and compromise
Are surely what's best when the baby cries?

Valerie Sutton

LOVE LETTER
(Dedicated to actress Beryl Reid)

Dear Tracey, I'll never forget last night.
You let me touch your things.
I've never explored up there before,
Well, only with Lizzie Springs.
But Lizzie Springs doesn't count now,
Honest, I mean it, I do!
You let me do things she wouldn't,
Things she wouldn't pursue.
I know I pinched her popcorn once
And I did have a lick of her ripple,
But you let me share your Strawberry Fayre,
Plus a peep in the dark at your nipple.
I don't remember the movie much,
You kept doing things with your lolly.
I watched your tongue going up and then down,
I couldn't stop staring, I'm sorry.
Then on the way home you gave me your chips
And we moaned about homework and things.
You giggled when I mentioned Durex
And the grease went all down your chin.
We passed the park where it's ever so dark,
I've marked you ten out of ten.
You brushed and bumped my biro
Again and again and again!
Oh Tracey, I'm writing this here in the lave,
At least I get peace in the loo,
But they're ringing the bell and it's algebra next,
Oh I wish it was things with you!

Alan Pinnock

HARDRAW FORCE WATERFALL, NORTH YORKSHIRE

Gentle silence except for sound
of falling water
and birds preparing fro bed.

Captivating, spellbinding silence
as October afternoon
gives way to twilight
and then to dusk.

An autumn leaf floated in a quiet pool,
desperately trying to come to terms
with its new surroundings . . .
then trespassed, unwisely, into the current
and was carried away . . .
until, the end of time?

Her gentleness is overwhelming.
He is alive again!
Apart from his family
he lives only for her.
They exchange the same greeting,
'I love you!'

They hug ever closer
despite fleece and walking boots.
It is a golden moment in the gentle silence
of an October afternoon . . .

Kinsman Clive

SONOROUS - THE VOICE THAT SOOTHES

The instant you came
My world began
For in moment of need
You appeared
From nowhere.
Your words were a balm to my ache,
They soothed my heart,
So aching it was
Deep down, it was gone
I thought.
Your advent
At that dreadful time
Turned all upheaval
Into tranquillity.
Indeed,
A comforter you are.
My gratitude knows no bounds,
So sonorous the voice
Vibrating, resounding
Deep to my ears,
Strengthening and refreshing,
That all will be well,
Indeed all is well,
In serenity my life lives.

Yemi Oyadiran

AN UNUSUAL FRIENDSHIP

We met in exceptional circumstance
On a German lorry, after the rout of France.
Towards the end of July, nineteen-forty.
He, a gentleman in his mid fifties,
I, a raw youngster approaching twenty.

'You seem to be down in the doldrums,' he said.
'Yes, my father's whereabouts unknown,
Our home was plundered by the invading Germans,
While the family was ordered on evacuation,
With Stukas and Panzers our constant companions.'

He agreed my plight was bad enough,
But added, 'It helps to remember
That no situation in life is ever so rough
That it could not have been much worse.'
He's right, I thought. After all, we're alive.

These wise words were the beginning
Of a lifelong friendship for Mr Roberts and me -
We were British civilians, captured in Northern France.
He, an area chief of the War Graves Commission,
I, keen to learn about the ways of the world.

Through ups and downs of internment,
Mr Roberts and I became more than friends.
We were looked upon by others as father and son.
He, always keen to share his experience of life.
I, always eager to plug any gaps in my education.

Alas, Mr Roberts is no longer of this world;
Within me, however, his indomitable spirit lives on.
His genuine qualities, in the Kipling mould,
His seeking for the real truths, always bold,
Have made of me, the person that I am from now on.

Andrew Cox

LEON

Twenty-one years I have known you
Twenty-one years today
From your very first frown, when you first looked around
To your smile, that can brighten my day
You are gentle and strong, stubborn and kind
It's just your memory that God left behind
Whatever the problem, whatever the strife
I'll always trust you to handle your life.
So my message today, is continue to be
One of the best things that happened to me.

Pat McCalvey

ELLIE
(Dedicated to my cousin Michelle)

When you call
The air is lighter
With sun shining through
The clouds of winter,
It brightens up a dull day
When memories of you
Are never far away.
They take me back
To happy times,
Of carefree days
When we were fine,
Playing 'til dark
With no problems to share,
Of the troubles ahead
We were unaware.
Now you have called
And brought it all back,
A smile's on my face,
We are back on track.

D Miller

YOU MAKE OUR DAY

Good morning everybody, the day has dawned so bright,
Another lovely morning, a long time till it's night.
Come on, get up, start playing, throw open the back door,
Draw back the kitchen curtains, let the sunshine in once more.
Then after we've had breakfast, it's off to play at ball,
Run amongst the trees and shrubs and hear old nature call,
To feel the wind blow through my fur and watch the squirrels run,
Oh hurry please, the river calls and swimming's so much fun.

Back home now in the garden, the afternoon has come,
I've had my lunch, a little nap, it's time now for more fun.
My life is full and happy, so much to learn and see,
I love my family dearly, the same as they love me,
But night is drawing in now, I've eaten all my tea;
My toys are all around the floor, it's sleepy-byes for me.
My bed is down and waiting, my pillow soft and warm,
Night, night, God bless to everyone, sweet dreams until the dawn.

K Townsley

JAZZ CLUB

House lights dim as music begins & conversational murmurs
are muted. Jazz quintet swings out a familiar tune from yesteryear - a
beat our feet feel as they begin to tap & fingers snap while heads bob in
twos & fours. Expert hands play the piano – left deftly creating full
chords as right magically melds melody.

We hum along & smile at memories. Tenor sax moans a reedy wail
through an *ad lib* chorus and room goes wild. Young folks explode with
applause as we do an old jitter-bug dance by our table. We sneak a
quick hug & then we sit - laughing while catching our breath.

Standup bass and drums exchange fours while piano carries tune. Back
& forth they duel - each vying to gain crowds' approval. Drummer
shows well - but inventive bassist crosses bridge and wins. We look into
each other's eyes & remember when.

Triple-tonguing trumpet tears a brassy riff as solo takes off. Quintet fills
behind & room roars with a standing ovation. Sixteen measures in -
music stops short. Horn plays intro for 'Call Of The Bulls' & drums
kick Latin beat – piano runs tune while all players play rhythm -
congas/bongos/claves & timbales.

Complex Caribbean cadence digs into soul - just too much - no one can
sit still. We do Salsa steps - hot! - hot! - hot! Fire flashing eyes send
secret messages & we rest again as song ends with crowd standing in
acclamation.

Session ends with lingering strains of - 'I've Got You Under My Skin.'
She leans head on my shoulder. Hand in hand we walk out in meter
with music melting us into passions almost forgotten.

Edward L Smith & Carmen M Pursifull

THAT SPECIAL MOMENT

Shimmering in a summer haze
Soda pop and ice cream days
That summer seemed to last forever
Bringing all our love together
Hope it never slips away
Hope I never see that day
Never see that day

Like the spiral in my dreams
I couldn't climb before
Through every twist and turn - I see
You open every door
To weave a magic web
Spinning love around my head
Gentle, peaceful shores
I'm not afraid anymore

It was a happening
That only love could bring
As the holiday drifts in time
We bring it back to life
Strange how it all behaves
That special moment will always stay
Never fading out of view
Always there for me and you.

Frank Howarth-Hynes

PASSING SWANS

Serene white swans upon the flowing tide
Recline their supple necks and, preening, glide,
Orange-billed, black-eyed,
In quiet array. Dark ripples chafe beside
The harbour wall as screaming seagulls chide,
Raucously deride
The graceful swans. Unruffled, dignified,
They arch their creamy, slender necks, to hide
Noble heads inside
Soft-feathered wings of milk-white down or, slide
Their sinuous forms beneath the sea. In wide
Arcs, as breasts collide
With white-flecked waves, whose curving wakes divide,
The cleaving swans pass by in stately pride.

John M Beazley

MEDITATION CLASS

We go there to seek peacefulness,
a retreat from the burdens that plague
our everyday lives with their complexity.

Sitting together in the class,
we exchange pleasantries and smiles,
anticipating the arrival of our teacher.

She appears and greets us warmly.
Her tales of innocence and experience
enrich our reflections and imaginings.

Now comes the request for silence:
we straighten our backs, bow our heads,
close our eyelids and count the rhythms of our breath.

We are asked to imagine a blue, healing light
flowing from the top of our bodies,
through to our solar plexus and down to our feet.

We visualise an energy force
journeying into our inner selves,
with a deft and imperceptible motion.

The stillness is so profoundly exquisite.
It enables us to search for spaces
amidst the distracting, obscured thoughts.

After only a short while,
we hear a voice telling us
to prepare for the end of our contemplations.

We slowly open our eyes,
which bask in the waves of tranquillity
pervading the room.

Julius Howard

OUR CUP WE RAISE

Those happy summer days,
Our cup we raise
A blessing to bestow,
In the soft, warm glow
Of the brilliant sun in June.
It blazes at noon.
The fields and meadows
Are bathed in a wonderful light,
As the hot sun burns so bright.
Night comes and the stars shine
A summer's night is gentle and sublime.
With a mild wind and balm,
Over the earth is a still calm.

I T Hoggan

MY BLUE KALEIDOSCOPE WITH FACETS

Glistening from the frozen window, as the bright sun is fighting to
peer through,
This makes me bright and happy, after long lapses of rain.
Whilst lying on my pillow drinking in its rays,
Folding my hands in a clasp and resting them on the chin,
I stare into the bright sapphire, that gives me such delight.
The magic of the sun melting ice is right within my sapphire gems,
The stones are now posed and are all of different shapes,
How they are fan-shaped, just as the peacock's tail.
I hold onto same position, with slight movement of a finger
The window is full blown and changes with every quiver,
My very own kaleidoscope, that is a magic gift,
A gift of Thai sapphires to Phillopiena, American lady poet.
They became a gift again to an Irish colleen with a classical
Greek name,
Living by a mystical brook in beautiful Wales.
This takes me back in time, whilst on my knees in prayer,
Peering through a diamond, a vision I did see that left me frozen.
It was the Virgin Mary, finely clad, with her infant on her lap.
On looking up the mystery solved, there she was in front of me
In all her glory in a wonderful stained glass window.

Margaret Gleeson Spanos

THE WOODLANDS

Early one November day,
We passed through the woodlands,
Following the shy deer trails, soundlessly walking,
Smelling the damp decay
Of rotten roots, earth and leaf mould.
The fog creeps through,
Mysterious mists of silence,
Add to our moods of sadness.
Where will we be by nightfall,
Choosing a new destiny, new land,
Hopeful of a welcome, a new peace.

Spiders' webs dangle dripping
With diamonds - dew,
Magnificent fungi, dangerous food,
Pre-historic filmy ferns bedded
In pillows of emerald moss
Fallen trees, death by natural causes
We cannot know what is in store,
Life's chances, life's adventures,
Life.

Leaving behind brutality,
Wars for supremacy - evil deeds
No respect for lives of another creed or race.
The dense woodland hid us, became our
Protector, friend and helper,
Healing us with its beauty and regrowth
Feeding us with berries and nuts,
Blessing us with the clear stream,
We travel on, weary, frightened
Reaching the edge of this woodland,
We reach our safe haven,
Another country, different, tolerances,
A second chance of decent life.

Margaret Ellis

A MOMENT IN TIME

That moment in the garden
You stop listening to the birds
See the wrens flitting in the trees
You don't realise how long you stood and watched

Then they all flew away
You walk back to the house contented
The mobile had rung 17 times
Back to reality

But it was worth it.

Carole A Cleverdon

SPECIAL MOMENTS

I'd love you to see how my baby eats an orange.
The concentration as she peels it,
The words she uses to describe it,
Her face when she drops it . . .
I'd love you to hear the way my baby chatters.
When she's talking about what she's seeing,
Enjoying what she's touching,
Happy in exploring, the frightening possibilities.
I'd love you to see the way my baby's smiling,
But the thought of my love for her
Just makes me break down and cry.
Tears from a stream that's never going to dry.

Anna B

DIDN'T YOU SEE ME ON THE TELLY?

Throughout the Golden Jubilee
From the first to the fourth of the month,
A million spectators thronged the Mall
And I was the million and oneth.

Under Admiralty Arch, close to Horseguards' Parade,
I unfurled my Union Jack
And I waved it and waved it for days and days -
'Twas the tiny wee flag at the back.

The Palace, away at the end of the Mall,
Had apparently - mysteriously - shrunk
To less than the size of a second-class stamp -
Perhaps caused by the champagne I'd drunk?

A discernible speck in the west was the Queen -
She could not have got very much smaller -
With beside her, her consort, Prince Philip, the Duke,
Like an atom, but fractionally taller.

Via speakers and screens I could almost take part -
Pomp and Circumstance, Zadok the Priest.
Though the Royals were wee indeterminate dots,
I could hear both the Eltons at least.

And such fireworks! Tremendous! A glorious display -
Cascading crescendos of light.
The Red Arrows and Concorde the following day
Almost equalled the previous night.

Human rainbows, huge butterflies, jigged down the Mall,
With St James's like springtime in Rio
And spectacular floats trooped the colour and all -
Even nannies with prams - passed *con brio.*

I stood cheering and waving my wee Union Jack -
And I swear, in the distance, Her Majesty waved back.

Norman Bissett

DELL-LIGHT

The fairies have been
In my garden
Again.
There was dew
Upon the gate.
There it shone
Bright silver, clear
Before all asleep
Were awake.
Their curtains of lace
By the spider borne
Adorned the fence
'Round the garden
Lawn.
Their music had been
The song of the birds.
Such pure delight
Without utter
Of words.
Their place of safety,
For no eyes to see,
The deep green ivy
'Neath the elderflower tree.
Then as the sun
Came to climb
The blue sky,
And shine its warmth
In the air to dry,
The mist that had held
The magic of dawn,
Left without trace
Of that
Fairy tale
Morn'.

Lyn Sandford

OUR WEDDING DAY

A bright spring morning
Greeted my wakening eyes
The buzz of chatter reached my ears
On this our wedding day

Up and about no rushing here
Lots of people to clean and prine
Coming and going but always calm
On this our wedding day

As people leave for the church
Our dresses we girls don
With tears in his eyes, Dad straightens his tie
On this our wedding day

The sky's now grey as the church appears
The wind is blowing too
But just inside I know you wait
On this our wedding day

Down the aisle we all glide
Through waves of white and mint
To say 'I do' in front of all
On this our wedding day

No nerves, no fears
Only excitement and joy,
And a love I know is true, waits for me
On this our wedding day

All the tears are gone
Now hearts full of joy,
Prepare to dance the night away
On this our wedding day

Now it's dark, our car is here
The time to leave has come
Our families remain to party on
As we leave to begin our life as one
On this our wedding day

Agnes Neeson

CLIMBING THE CHURCH TOWER

'One hundred and twenty-three steps,'
Said the man down below.
Seems like a thousand and twenty-three,
Winding, worn and narrow.
One side, a brass rail to clutch,
The other, a crumbling wall.
Few alcoves for resting;
As we go higher, none at all.
At last an ancient splintered door
Leads to fresh air.
Out of breath, throats aching,
But we're there.
I cough, splutter,
And admire the views of the town.
Seems a lot easier
Coming down.

Julia Perren

ANGEL

I watched in awe and wonder
As my daughter gave birth to you
The minute you came into this world
You were a dream come true.
Your little hands were closed so tight
As if trying to hold on
To something safe that felt secure
Something, you thrived upon.
Your mum looked tired and weary
As she held you close to her
And looked into your tiny face
Not believing you were there.
I felt a tear run down my cheek
As my heart it did remember
How I once lay upon a bed
Your mum and me together.
So Brooklyn, when you are old enough
Just know that this is true
The minute you came into this world
An angel was born too.

Elaine Davidson

DAWN

Dawn steals across the land.
Barely perceptible at first.
The night, a lesser shade of blue,
Blue to bland, then suddenly a ray of light.
Which shatters the silence of the night.
Blue now becomes a ruddy hue,
Setting the dawn clouds aglow
Like streaks of blood
Soaking into newly, fallen snow.
Then the sun's sanguine globe,
Transmutes to one of gold.
As if orchestrated by an alchemist of old.
And so the dawn world unfolds,
Sun fully risen on its journey to the west.
Bright beams of light break into our dreams.
Stir our thoughts to consciousness,
To rouse us from our nightly rest, refreshed.

Jonathan Pegg

CHILDHOOD MEMORIES

So many memories flicker through my mind
Days by the seaside, bucket and spade,
Walks in the nearby forests with no thought of disaster.
Bluebells not picked, just looked at with gleeful eye,
A pleasure boat on the river to brighten our day.
Picnic teas in the park on a bright summer day at 4pm.
Old fashioned flowers adorn the front garden,
The back garden, full of organic, wholesome vegetables.
Trainspotters at the local station in full swing
Numbers taken down in a scrappy note book,
Albums full of delightful scraps
Bought at the corner shop for a penny.
A place of variety on all different items,
Many eyes espied chocolates in the sweet shop window,
The local bobby would come along
Slap each one of us with his gloves
Around the head and we laughed it
All off, when he had moved us on.
Going to the local theatre with Mum and Dad
Comedians made us laugh
An ice cream at the interval made mostly by custard powder
Home at last in a very merry mood.
Those were the days when life ticked over slowly
One had time to think and be joyful.
No worries, money was low but,
It seemed to go round and still a little
Money was left over for a merry fling,
At the end of the week.

Alma Montgomery Frank

MY FRIEND EILEEN

I met my friend Eileen many years ago
She was the friend I always wished I had,
We met in Germany, we were both army wives
She came round for a coffee and a chat
With her two children, we both had different lives.

Our husbands went away often, we'd help each other out.
We took the good days with the bad when the kids played up,
We'd scream and shout.
The months came and went, sharing walks,
Having suppers and teas for the kids.

We'd go off to the outdoor pool for the day
Pack the bags, make the sandwiches
All we had to buy was a bag o'chips.

We had good nights out and good nights in,
These good girlie nights really saved our skin.
Let's go round the Shnelly, get some chicken and potato salad,
It made our mouths water, and chewing the crispy bits for a long
time after.

We had a go at acting, making our wigs,
Wearing the boots, we had all the gear, even the voice!
Oh, we did get some funny looks!

We were up there on the stage, plenty of Dutch courage, I may add
We wouldn't have been up there long, we even gave them a song.
Good fun was had by all, wearing those boots -
We were doing our Max Wall.
Then it was all over and we felt quite glad
But to see it all finish, we felt rather sad.

The men went away a lot, but we just muddled through
Both of us together, our friendship just grew and grew,

We made the long trip home when the men went away for a long spell
The suitcases, the bags, the pushchair, then on the plane and on
                                                    the train, oh it was hell!
The kids were so young then, we all travelled a long way,
But we all just got on with it, going home to Mum
Somewhere different to stay.

All that was a few years ago, but the memories are oh so clear
We parted for a while, things went a bit wrong,
But we're back together, friends again
Because to me, my friend Eileen is ever so, ever so, dear.

Marie Edwards

My Children

I have six children, two girls, four boys,
Their moment of birth was something so pure,
Each little one and their cry for life,
Their little fists flying as they prepared to fight,
Each birth was so different,
But the feelings never changed,
A love so overwhelming, to protect and keep safe.

The ups and downs of life we had,
But got through it with a smile,
My children went from little to big,
Through teenage years, sometimes with tears,
But they made it, all six of them.

Looking back on my life, would I change anything?
Some things I might,
But not my children, not one single thing,
They have been my life, my reason to live,
Without them my life would have been just,
Black and white,
With them, a rainbow, a rainbow so bright,
These are my children who I've loved all my life,
Joseph and Alan, Azra and Sal, Aaron and Jay.

Mary Neill

THE RETURN

I returned to the gentle hills,
And stood once again in the green, peaceful valley,
Where the tall trees watch,
By the silver lakes
Where the kingfisher darts.

In the cool of a still August evening,
The tranquil peace of the water
Reflected the fleecy clouds, as they drifted
Over the silver lakes
Where the kingfisher darts.

I watched the ducks leisurely preening;
No sound broke the golden silence,
As the tall trees stood by the still waters
Of the silver lakes,
Where the kingfisher darts.

As gentle as the soft touch of a whisper,
The trickling water caressed the weir,
While the house in the distance looked down
Through the watching trees
To where the kingfisher darts.

Some part of me will forever remain here
In the peaceful valley,
With the watchful trees, giving shade
By the silver lakes,
Where the kingfisher darts.

Joan Thompson

JARRED'S POEM

As you come
Into the world
And see it all around
Every smell, every sight
Every little sound
To you, my dear
It seems so new
To your wondering eyes
But rest assured my precious child
Your eyes will never lie
When you sleep
Where do you go?
What wonders do you see?
A world of colour
Magic and toys
A world that never sleeps
Where you can play
With friends to us, unseen
You play forever safe
Watched by angels
In this world as you
Look around, awake
Safe in your parents'
Loving arms
Protected from all harm
To see the magic all around
To our precious son
May the angels keep you safe
And watch you whilst you sleep

Stephanie Grocott

SHYNESS

I cannot
Remember
When
I saw
You first
And then
Again
And caught
Your eye
And wonder
Why
I could
Not
See.

Nicola Barnes

A BOMBSHELL
(For: Dawn)

A foot soldier of life
Weary from the world
And its confrontational
Words of war.

In search of comfort
Seeking a friend's embrace.

Unknowingly . . .
Blind, with lack of sleep
Strayed into . . . into . . .
An emotional minefield.

Heart and head
Blown apart . . .
Still alive
Not quite dead.
Devastated
By a bombshell
Of what the friend
Just said,
'Imprisoned as we are by misfortune
Thankfully love keeps our spirits fed'.

Malcolm Peter Mansfield

COCAINE NIGHTS
(Inspired by J G Ballard)

White is the colour of silence
   The silence of private worlds
Secured from outside intervention
   By non-conformist intrusions
Where petty crime is tolerated
   And light pornography condoned
And the residents die of boredom
   Before their flower arranging's done.

Red is the colour of discord
   The discord of public domains
Open to external influences
   From uncontrollable elements
Where any rage is punished
   And all smuttiness condemned
And the inhabitants live for freedom
   Instead of a day's work hard done.

Joe Loxton

MY SOUVENIRS

The good times I've had, long gone by
Like the first time I heard my baby cry
These precious moments I'm unlikely to forget
Stored too in my archive are some regrets
My mixed emotions, the joys and the fears
Scattered are they, amongst my souvenirs

My youth long passed, I've encapsulated
The beautiful maidens that I have dated
My conquests, my failures that I've endured
All deeply entombed and safely secured
Pressures encountered from day to day
Denies me the time to often pass this way

Today unlike others is special to me
Reflections unfolding, long-lost memories
Pictures I see flooding back in my mind
For them I'm so thankful, I've always been kind
For now I'll abandon all worries and cares
I'll revisit my past to view my souvenirs

Ainsley McKenzie

A SUNDAY IN NOVEMBER

Grève de Lecq woods
Not Delville, Mametz or Happy Valley.

Spent acorn rounds
And exploded chestnut cases.
Everything caked in mud.

We stand aside for two horses,
Riders in glistening capes,
And hang onto splintered sycamore
Branches. The path we walk
Through is a ditch,
Our feet sinking
Into soft mud.

Occasionally beneath our feet
We feel something firm;
They slip on smooth rocks.
We find a green bottle at the cross-roads.

Just before eleven
A young boy's cry
Echoes down the valley.

Rain strafes us unceasingly.
We bend our heads into the cold
And turn back, defeated,
Our mission unaccomplished,
The mud sucking at our boots.

As we emerge through the tunnel of trees
An armistice of sunbeams
Breaks through the clouds.

Alan G Jones

THE SEA AROUND ME

The unpredictable waves of God's great oceans
can tempt a heart to play.
The formidable wilderness of sea's expanse,
the familiar cry of the gulls

Oh what pleasure to ride on a boat upon the crest of ocean waves
The taste of salted seawater spray upon my face,
The vast expanse of ocean all around me
Some part of me set free.

To ride upon God's clear wide ocean, what joy that brought to me
For now I know the secret of the sailor, the fisherman too
For now I too have been humbled by the splendour of the vast,
formidable sea!

Viv Eckett

BATH

The snow fell in Bath today
and made a pretty sight.
The flakes came tumbling from the sky
and turned the city white.
It settled on the hillside,
where frost is often seen
and footprints down our garden path,
show where the postman's been.
It danced upon the rooftops,
where chimneys stand so high
and fell on ancient graveyards,
where sleeping folk do lie.
I hope the snow will fall again
another winter day
and stay around for all to see,
before it melts away.

Tom Clarke

SNOW MAIDENS

That morning,
I looked out,
and realised
that Persephone
had shot through
gone 'Down Under',
yet again.

Aurora,
drowsy redhead,
rose slowly
(too slow to catch a cold),
and cast
a little light
on the proceedings.

My footprints soiled
the virgin beds
of pillowed snow,
and rumpled
the billowed sheets,
heaped
in dazzling dunes -
a contrary Sahara.
Smoothed,
creaseless, colourless,
no highs or lows.

I crunched between
hidden hedgerows,
sinking
into cold chasms,
while a magpie
strutted his stuff
above me -
looking down
his Art-Deco nose,
at an albino pigeon
perched,
on a peeking stile.
Invisible,
apart from
a neon eye,
and his
'mobile phone' hellos.

I blinked
at the sun,
and the canvas
turned crimson.

Jennifer D Wootton

ST GEORGE'S DAY

Mesmerised, locked deep in rainbow eyes,
Fair maiden I am, transfixed by scales,
Poisoned breath and rank sweat swamping me,
Curled tongue licking, drooling jaws draw close,
Wings outstretched, writhing tail, daggered teeth.

I'd faint for this dragon, be devoured,
Bur Sir George arrives on hobby horse;
A plastic sword kills the cardboard box.
I kiss my hero to please the crowd.

Still I'd rather hug those lethal scales,
Feel hot dragon breath scar my pale skin.

Paula Holt

THE OTHER SIDE

Grim was the hour and dark the day
When she slipped quietly away;
A truer friend I'll never know,
Such anguish when I let her go;
    I'd agonised,
    I must be strong,
    she'd lingered here
    for far too long
Burdened by pain and in distress,
And shackled by my selfishness.

Then in the dark a brilliant light,
And there she was, so young and bright,
And from her new world soundlessly
She sent her gratitude to me;
    Then all at once
    the light had gone
    and Emily
    had journeyed on;
What peacefulness the vision brought,
She had not died as I had thought.

Bewildered yet, whene'er I try
It still eludes, the reason why
That revelation came to me,
It seemed that I'd been meant to see
    My dear old friend
    just one time more,
    she had returned
    yo reassure;
So privileged, so blessed that I'd
A chance to see the other side.

Hilary J Cairns

TEARS TO THE GODS

(Night, night my sweet love)

When I die, will you bury me in one of your tears
Of love as then will know that
Forever more, I will be surrounded
By your love.

I will carry your tear of love to the gods of love
To show them I am not carrying a tear of sorrow,
I am carrying a tear of love that you gave to me
To keep our love from the wolves of darkness.

When I die will you bury me in one of your tears
Of love, as I will know that the gods of love will keep
The wolves of darkness from our love so that the
Tears of sorrow that are in your eyes will fade away.

As the door of life will open for you to find
That your heart still has a love for life.

I have given you my tear of love, to keep
The wolves of darkness from our love
For us to meet once again in the
Hands of the gods of love.

Until then, my love, I will leave you
With my tear of love so it will bring
My love to you
Every time you blow me a kiss.
Until we meet once again
In the hands of the gods of love
For me to say to you my love,

'Night, night my sweet love.'

Paul Wilcox

OUR LAST GOODBYE

I went to visit my mum one day
As she hadn't been too well, they say.
It was a lovely room she had
But sometimes she was so sad.

On this day we were the closest
Holding her hand, Mum was grand.
We chatted about childhood days
'I love you Mum,' I just had to say.

When growing old, you see things,
Like Mum, remembering when she was young.
But, hey, we are having a lovely day
There isn't much more I can say.

On leaving her, she gave me a hug
Not like Mum, as we kissed goodbye,
My mum sat in her usual chair
I went off, totally unaware.

Before I left, I looked up and saw
Mum standing on her balcony,
She blew me a kiss and whispered goodbye.
How did she get there? I wondered why?

Two days later my dear mum died.
All I did was cry and cry.
But when I thought, hey, how strong she was,
And we'd shared our last goodbye.

J P Dawe

GOD BLESS THE . . . CORRS

Baptism is a solemn affair.
Of this my granddaughter Anja was blissfully unaware.
In her cream silk dress looking like a regal seraphim she was
entranced by all the pomp, her love of music knew no bounds as the
congregation stood to sing the hymns, up on her sturdy legs she stood
and 'la-la-la'd', head-banged and stomped.
'Breathless' by the Corrs is her favourite tune, to this she laughs
and dances with glee.
The kindly vicar smiles, and nods for all his congregation to see.
Unfalteringly he continues Jesus' story to be told as Anja in her
innocence has broken the mould.
Young and old smiled at her as she 'sang' and waved to me, surely up
in Heaven celestial bells rang at this tot oblivious of the
solemnity dancing with glee?
She was duly baptised. 'Anja Taylor Hefti'. We all shed a tear.
Would she remember her 'Nonno' from Switzerland adoringly singing
a solo for her and wishing that he lived a little nearer?
If only she could stay as she is today, without fear, no hatred
to harm her, to not be afraid of the dark, to keep forever that
vitality, that spark. Looking through those clear blue eyes for the
goodness in people which surely lurks there, hidden through doubt
of fear, somewhere.
We pray for her happiness, her health and prosperity and that her
kindness will make her glow as safe in our love she will grow.
The service is ended as the cub scouts parade out of the huge old
oak doors, Anja is still waving.
My daughter's tear-filled eyes meet mine then we hug and whisper,
'God bless the . . . 'Corrs'!'

J M Hefti-Whitney

CHACOMBE

Breton bed, wood and linen,
Fierce possessive kisses,
We undress our love
Blinded by tears.

A red rose, silk and paper,
Making your reflection,
Ribbons shed
Golden hoops shrinking.

Candlelight, moon promises
Ripples breaking on the shore
Scented fingers
Taste divine.

Emma Jane Stroud

HANNAH AND MARK'S WEDDING CELEBRATIONS

In Trinity Mews it was night,
and Chucky and Edward - the hamsters
were playing in the moonlight
for their master and mistress would be celebrating
their marriage on the morrow
and for them that was no sorrow
but more seed to eat and water to drink
and for master and mistress
their pens would be wet with ink.

Hannah and Mark are to sign the register
and perhaps they might travel to Leicester
for Hannah comes from Birmingham and
she loves the Black Country but both her
and Mark like Ireland
to sample the Guinness from the River Liffey
not so silly.
Their reception will be like a Westend production
that night of nights
where Hannah in her crimson velveteen gown
will capture Mark in his bespoke town.
Hannah and Mark will be happy,
though there will be times when both become a little snappy
but Chucky and Edward will play and play
for another day,
when Hannah and Mark their vows exchanged will love
each other to produce a child
boy or girl it matters little
happiness will be complete
as these little children grow to be model
siblings of their parents' glow.
God bless you Hannah, God bless you Mark
you have made a splendid start.

Gerard Allardyce

MOTHER IS COMING FOR CHRISTMAS

Daughter: 'Mother's coming for Christmas,' I carol,
                 and watch the children's faces change.
                 'Who wants Granny? She's old!
                 She's fussy! She's a party pooper!'

Grandmother: Help, it's Christmas again!
                 I suppose I'll have to go!
                 And put up with the noise,
                 too much food and indigestion!
                 I'd much rather stay at home.

Daughter: 'My dears, Grandma is not so bad,
                 she will be here for a few days!
                 Surely you can practise a little tolerance?
                 For my sake, if not for a better reason.
                 After all, it's only a short visit!'

Grandmother: I'm too old for all this upheaval!
                 I'd like to stay here and watch TV,
                 doze in my chair and wake up ratty!
                 Eat what I like and that's not much,
                 go to bed early, or doze in my chair.

Daughter: 'My dears, remember it's *Christmas*,
                 the time for love and good will.
                 She's old, she's lonely, you know!
                 She loves coming home to see you all,
                 and - this year, might be her last!'

Grandmother: Oh well! I suppose I'd better go
                 or everyone will be disappointed.
                 I'll make it plain, I'm only staying
                 for a day or two. Maybe I'll make it three!
                 After all, I am my daughter's mother!

Christabell Bull

ON THIS SPECIAL DAY

Coral anemones in crevices of the rockpools
Quite unafraid of the sea's different moods,
Cling to the slippery sides of granite,
Like full-blown chrysanthemums.
This special day are watched by Kate and Sarah and me,
Are gazed upon in wonder and quiet philosophy.
And all around the relics of the sea lie ready to be gathered up.
Empty old crab shells painted orange and red
Encrusted seaweed dry and silvered
Sits amongst the myriad coloured pebbles,
And the red patterned rocks, inscribed with fishermen's nets.
For a moment looking up from the shore to the grassy slopes of cliff,
Pale primroses and early purple orchids splash their patches of colour
Onto the fresh spring grass.
On this special day
The flat, calm sea mirrors the sitting seagulls,
And creates such peace and such contentment,
That for a space of time all the problems of this troubled world
Are quite forgotten.
No Falkland crisis here, no family sickness,
The flat, calm sea
The sound of tiny waves running up the shore,
Eliminates anxieties from the mind,
Brings relaxation and happiness so deep and full
In this sweet company.

K M Brown

ONE MOMENT

That one moment
I searched for
And finally found.

That one moment
I longed for
And shook through the sound.

That one moment
I begged for
And began to feel whole.

That one moment
I felt for
And forgot the truth of my soul.

That one moment
I will remember
And regret it wasn't with her.

Benjamin Carr

BOY IN A BALACLAVA

Icicles on barrack roofs.
Stacking toys in a store room
Off a smoke-filled mess hall.
Photographs with refugee children.

The laughing brown-eyed boy
In bright blue boots and balaclava,
Too young to know a proper home,
I could have hugged and brought to mine.

Joyce Walker

LISBON

Wide-open bay and the largest bridge in Europe,
Motorways and tolls,
Many Embassy buildings,
Showing off different styles,
Part of an old fortress by the water's edge,
Monuments of many kinds,
Woodlands through the centre of the city,
Many squares,
A fine parliament building and old palaces,
Before my eyes a monastery built
Long ago for sailors to call in before
They departed on long voyages at sea,
A building very large, containing many
Works of art, alas a large number
Of stones need to be replaced,
Monarchs of old lay in crypts within her walls.

G F Snook

WARTIME CHILD

Those sirens blasted their sad lament, to warn of enemies' approach
Guns roared, shrapnel fell, the air was filled with smoke
Those enemy planes hovered overhead and discharged
                              what they had brought
Bombs to eradicate the city and kill innocent folk
We in our basement shelter, too nervous to speak or joke
Emerging at the end of the all-clear, we dismally gazed around
Where once was grace and beauty, rubble littered the ground
A dreadful taste was on the air, it made all cough and sneeze
We all suffered from reddened eyes for many a long day
                              as that foul enemy teased
No home, no clothes, no food, despair loomed, darkness
                              evaded everywhere
Like sheep we were herded by special auxiliary wardens
To derelict halls and vacated classrooms, soup was distributed
                              from giant cans
We greedily took what was offered, there was no grace to be said
We washed in luke-warm water and was shown a mattress bed
Poor Mother in a persistent daze had to be led about
Eventually she had to leave to be hospitalised no doubt
Those air-raid warnings came so often, we appeared to get
                              used to them
We attended makeshift lessons and were counted just like hens
All families lived and shared together, all got on considerably well
Sharing and caring companionably, we children thought this 'swell'
Eventually this idyllic style of life was threatened and we all
                              were sent away
Miles out in the country, Mother had died, we were sad, sorry to say
We received the love and kindness of smashing foster folk as
                              they cherished this brood of four,
The authorities wanted to part us but we stuck together during
                              this dreadful war

ROYAL OCCASION

With hat and gloves so fitting to this very British occasion
My royal garden party invite is checked and double checked
A visit to Buckingham Palace whether invited or paying to visit
Can only be experienced once with excitement
Money now being able to buy
A glimpse of this magical palace and gardens
So with pride of being British and full of respect
The taking of tea with a host of ladies and gentlemen
With some in uniform to add to the occasion
With added glimpse of our royal family
The feeling of being privileged is one all can feel
When invited to a garden party

Janet Glew

CHILDHOOD RECOLLECTIONS

Those childhood days,
Full of adventure,
Explorers in pursuit of our dreams.
Every day as exciting as the one before.
Always together,
Hiding, seeking,
Finding treasure of old.
Climbing trees, ghost hunting,
Being scared, being bold.

A friendship, a bond,
From Heaven it was sent.
Creating mischief and laughter,
Wherever we went.

Having picnics, going swimming,
Doing projects together.
Listening to music, reading books,
Together, whatever the weather.

Childhood recollections
Swirl in my heart.
From years of fabulous fun.
A stitch in time.
That is alone mine.
My special cloak of happiness.

Donna Salisbury

BLACKPOOL ROCKS
(Dedicated to Mum, Dad, Ian, Allan, Tom, Chloe, Rhys and Harry)

These are the days,
I sit back and enjoy.
There's no time like the present,
To sit down and look back.

The best holiday ever,
A special moment in our past.
Something we all have in common,
No cares in the world.

We all got on with each other,
No arguments or tears.
The sun was shining, the skies were blue,
The air so fresh and windy.

Roller coaster rides, Dinky Donuts,
2p slot machines and we were happy.
All of us together, the one thing we all know is
That *Blackpool rocks!*

The tower, the waxworks,
Each pier and arcade.
We saw them all,
In the warm sunny September of 2002.

Emma Barker

THE LOVE KNOWN IS NOT RECEIVED

Walking her highway, the lady's on her own,
searching for a love that she can call her own.

Fell in love too easily and often paid the price.
A lonely relationship, another lonely night.

She had given up on being anyone's wife.
She'd walk her highway and just live her life.

And she had given up on looking for a love
to fit within her heart like a hand within a glove.

But then she met a friend and he moved closer.
She liked what she saw and let him come nearer.

He showed her a passion that warmed her soul,
he showed her touch and made her feel whole.

She gave in return her love from an open heart,
knowing the dangers, knowing they would part.

The love she felt was good, she felt so alive.
It felt so right to love him and make him sigh.

Now he's told her goodbye, so sorry, he's got to go.
She's once more on her own and so sad to see him go.

Her heart is not broken, it was not his to burn.
She gave openly, looking for nothing in return.

She learned a lesson, the greatest she's been given.
The love known is not received, it is what's given.

Angela G Pearson

NATIVITY PLAY
(For Ellie)

There she was, only six,
At the back of the stage,
Proud to be one of the angels,
And I, nearer sixty and equally proud,
Tossed her a wink which she caught
And returned with a smile so sweet
I swear
All Heaven lit up for that moment
And melted, like me.

Alan Millard

OUR GOLDEN DAYS

Those precious golden days
When you and I lived just for the moment
Reaching out with open arms to
The rapture and joy of our love.
Young, vital, alive and free as the birds,
Together we explored the steep craggy hills
With the biting wind in our faces
Catching our words - 'Darling I love you'.
Running, climbing, clinging to our every embrace
In sheer delight, happy and carefree.

Those precious golden hours
When time stood still
And in a world of our own
We lived and cherished every minute
Caring, loving and sharing our hearts' desires.
Only God knows and understands our ecstasy
Which can never be taken away
They belong only to you and I,
Treasured memories locked deep
In our hearts for all eternity.

Was it just a dream we shared?
Now it all seems beyond our reach.
Yet in moments of loneliness and pain
When days are filled with uncertainty,
Memories are stirred and like fire embers
They rekindle into a living, burning glow
Setting our very souls aflame with joy,
Knowing we have lived a lifetime together
In only a few God-given hours,
For ever remaining 'our golden days'.

Joy Schelling

TENDER MOMENTS

Your soft lips and your perfume,
The sunlight in your hair
So many happy moments
Only you and I could share

The way we held hands and walked together
Every day was summertime
Even on cold winter days
I felt love's glow

I loved those tender moments
I used to spend with you
Those warm and loving moments
That only we both knew

I loved those tender moments
When into each other's eyes we stared
So much love was spoken
But not from lips that cared

I loved those tender moments
When we spoke in undertones
When I told you you were beautiful
And we let our loving tones

I loved those tender moments
When our arms were lovingly entwined
When our bodies yearned to be together
With your lips pressed close to mine

B Page

THE NIGHT OF MY LIFE

You told me to close my eyes,
You had something to give me,
A special gift for us to share.

I closed my eyes,
Kept them very tightly shut,
Wondering what the big surprise was.

You said I could open my eyes,
And all I could see was
A bright shiny diamond staring back at me.

Your hands were shaking
As you got down on one knee,
I knew you were going to ask to marry me.

I had no hesitation
To say yes to my true love,
Now we are committed, we show our love.

You've made me so happy,
I'm so glad you are near,
This moment is one I'll never forget.

Thank you dear Peter
For being the one,
And thank you for loving me
No matter what.

Lisa-Jane Clarke

SPECIAL MOMENTS

If not for you,
Where would I be?
You give me strength,
To see me through.
If not for you,
There would be no charm,
My world would not be as warm without you.

Ann Lacy

PERFECT CHANCE

I found him there,
With a gun to his face.
Trying to lose,
The human race.
With a pull and a click,
The hammer was cocked,
As the lightning flashed,
Our eyes were locked.

I felt his grief,
I heard his pain,
I even heard
The ex-girlfriend's name.
He cussed it once,
He cried it twice,
Before I could stop him,
Fate rolled the dice.

I saw myself in him,
As the corpse hit the floor,
I picked up the gun
And put it to my jaw.
I imagined myself,
Putting blood on the floor.
But it just wasn't me,
To fate I'm a whore.

Dhan Whitelock

SPECIAL MOMENTS

With the turn of the old year
and fresh opening of the new
comes the joy of family love;
Of giving and receiving;
of sharing food and merriment;
of thoughts and experiences.
We gather together from far and near
to renew our bonding, to spread good cheer.
All these moments are special,
but some touch the heart.
Times when we meet with the future,
in the lovely faces of our new family members,
our new great-grandchildren.
In these moments we feel ourselves a part
of the abiding history of our family
fresh branches on the family tree.
We hold them in our arms, and pray
that they be blessed and guided on the way.
That the world and life be kind, and give them space.
That they will grow and prosper
in God's everlasting grace.

Mary Johnson-Riley

SNOW

Someone spread a blanket
Over the Earth today.
A gentle blanket of purest white.
Woven so fine on the loom last night.
Edged with a silk of satin grey.
Who spread the blanket
Over the Earth today?

Clare Todd

I'M DREAMING

I'm lying dreaming of an angel
From Heaven above
I'm lying dreaming of an angel
To hold tenderly and love
For the whole of my long or short lifetime
On this war-torn world of ours

Her long golden hair
Flows so freely in the wind
Her angel blue eyes
Sparkle brighter than the stars
Her ruby-red lips are sweeter
Far sweeter than honey to kiss
And her slender angel's body
Feels so warm and tender in my arms
Every time I hold her closer and closer
To my heart

But in reality will it ever
Will it ever come true?
That's why I'm lying dreaming
Of an angel like you
Of a beautiful angel like you Dianne
Of a beautiful angel like you

Donald John Tye

THE MOMENT I KNEW

The music played loudly, and there were lots of bodies closely together.
The smell of wine was in the air. We'd all had one too many.
It was the Christmas spirit.
There she was just a few metres away from me.
She danced with experience, and had eyes from everywhere on her.
While dancing I stared at her, and knew how much I admired her,
Wanted to be in her company.
But then she turned and our eyes met.
The music seemed to go quieter and into the background.
The fast-moving bodies seem to slow, the lights seemed to
                                              focus on her,
And for what must have been a few seconds, but felt like minutes
Became the most powerful moment of my life.
She looked at me, and just smiled from inside her heart.
I knew I was in love with her.
I knew I was in love with a woman.
The past few years all came together at that very moment.
It all made sense now.
I knew I was gay and had fallen head over heals.

Lynsey Tocker

HENRIETTA

They were busy that day, when it happened.
That truly wonderful thing.

I was about seven at the time, and it was my job
to run and check to see if the birth had begun.

It was one of those mundane things, you know
twenty trips . . . nothing.

And then . . .

I opened the door, and there she lay looking at me with them
blue, blue eyes. She grunted and I stood glued to the spot.

It was a feeling that has never left me, even to this day.

Two weeks later, as I stood in the straw in my wellies,
A tiny piglet was handed to me. Henrietta had a good pair
of lungs on her, I kissed and cuddled her and put her back to run
to her mum and her siblings.

Moira Jean Clelland

ARCADIAN INTERLUDE

Passing honeymooners, we never knew his name.
We christened him 'Specs', neat youth tending
tables at Arcadia, a crowded patisserie
displaying monochromes of stern men from the
old country: 'moustachioed Mafia' you said.

He moved flamenco-slim along the aisles, his
tray a precious salver; dared to toss and catch
it; frustrated discus thrower. Bifocals refracted
his knowing smile, no guile, fame never far ahead.

Collecting detritus, correcting chairs, he wiped
formica, transcending clients like a phantom.
Perhaps he saw ghosts of customers to come,
himself as proprietor of this menial world.
His nostril curled in Smoking and Kiddy Korner.

Unobsequious even with the posing patrons,
maybe he fancied he was patrician in another life,
his then wife at least a prima donna.
Crisp in white and black, his shoe sheen shamed
smocked counter girls who loved outskilling him,
'Must be killing him!' you whispered in farewell.

On our tenth anniversary you prompted our return,
coyly anticipating progress. 'Specs' still tended
tables; same smile, no guile, just ghosts ahead.
As if cued to glide outside, he did his tray trick,
'Discus thrower without a target,' you said.

Malcolm Williams

ALL THE TIME NOW

We came to be with you, share the time that we have,
today, just as always, understand good and bad.
We walked into you, you said we walked into us,
filled with resemblance, a place we can trust.
You and your caring, your love and your fear:
here right inside us, beside us and near.
Now there is everything , also, and all,
never be frightened, we know when you call.

There is solitude, empathy, solace and peace,
a picture that speaks to us, colours we reach,
telling our hearts what we all know is true:
a story that 'we' know and you know it too.
A shop and a window, a passage of time,
words without ending, worlds in the lines,
your intricate workings of life on the edge,
fitting in tapestries, all in our heads.

We wonder how 'you' know, but we don't have to think,
you and your voice are the pen and the ink,
keeping us filled with a spiritual dream,
all of your seeing unspoken is seen,
blood to the dying, sight to the blind,
brothers and sisters, a joining of kind,
floating in cosmos, mystery friends,
never unbroken, never to mend.
You and your wisdom, and us in between,
believers of life share a beautiful scene,
a home with a healer who knows and has known,
walking as one into love as we go.

Maria Daines

HER LEGACY TO ME

If I had a time machine
I'd go right back in time,
To that special day we met
On that special chime.
Your eyes lit the unlit streets
And showed me how to see,
Your lips shared the caring words
Which today made me.
Your hands showed the gentle touch
Of silk and sheer delight,
Your body shared the wave-like movements
Which propped me so upright.
You shared your skills and tactful talents
That you had learnt in life,
Then you shared sad and happy balance
We need to get through life.
Most of all you shared me you
And taught me these lessons in life.

Alexander E Clarke

NEW LIFE

Life begins and keeps on beginning.
A birth is a time to celebrate.
From a mother a new life - a daughter or a son.
A daughter then brings new life again.
The memories all return
With a grandchild who brings joy.
Enjoyment as she grows
The change in a smile,
Movements of fingers or toes,
The cooing, the chatting,
Bright laughter she brings
As daily she grows
It makes you wonder where time goes.
As your family moves on
Generations of happiness
Through both young and old
Makes life worth living - a gift to behold.

Gwendoline Woodland

SPECIAL MOMENTS

'Okay Vivien, I'll leave you for another night
See you tomorrow sometime after nine-thirty
If you're worried in any way you have my phone number
Now remember, it doesn't matter what the time is
I'm always ready to be with you if needed.'

One-thirty and I'm awake in a flash
'Pains regular and quite strong.'
'Good, fetch the pack from the spare room
Plenty of hot water and I will be there in twenty minutes.'
The hall light flicked on as my car approached
'Sh!' said Tom. 'The boys are asleep.'
He took the gas and air machine and climbed the stairs
I unbuttoned my coat, my midwifery bag in the other hand

Foetal heart, blood pressure, pulse, fine
Contractions now stronger and regular
The feeling of trust and comradeship deepened
As the labour progressed in nature's best way

Tom sat holding her hand
His arm protectively curled around her head and shoulders
All three engaged in nature's miracle birth
Gently the head was eased out
Followed in a swoosh by the warm body
Safely encased in slippery liquid
It lay, a little girl attached to its mum
Clamps applied and the first separation took place
Pink face contorted by the mighty cry
Warmly wrapped in the new clean sheet
She was firmly clasped in her mother's welcoming arms
Her father gazing in wondrous amazement
The first daughter he had helped to produce

Frances Ann Hall

HAPPY MOMENTS

The waking of a brand new day,
The sun high in the sky,
Rain on the windowpane,
Snow falling from the sky.
Reading a brand new book,
Sitting by an open fire,
Being able to use my hands,
Walking about each day,
Things we take for granted,
These are all special things.
Watching my children grow,
The cat curled up by the fire,
The bark of a dog,
The birth of a lamb,
The sound of the birds singing,
The sensation of sound,
Grateful that I possess all senses,
While others have not.
Indeed when I think about it,
Special moments I have a lot.

Jane Margaret Isaac

MY ONE TRUE LOVE

The beauty that you possess
Both inside and out
From your twinkling eyes
To your gentle voice
With words so good to me
Lifting me to another world.

You turn and smile at me
My heart begins to burn
You take hold of my hand
My blood begins to boil
The love I have for you
Holds no barriers.

The grip between our hands loosen
You let go and you look
Deep into my eyes and you smile.
You begin to walk away
Until the next time we meet
I will be thinking of you.

Symmn Draw

SPECIAL MOMENT

Northern lights play
Over the muted land
So deep in snow.

As we cross the fields
In the sharp winter night
Your hand grasps mine
And love is warmth
Though the wind freezes the skin.

Now not far distant
The lights of home beam out
Across the snow.
I think of our small room
Lit by the flickering wood stove,
Where we will lie
In that sure embrace
Which heart cannot translate
Nor words endure.

Brenda Lismer

GIBRALTAR

The camps at Drumack and Dunaird were ready to receive
These lovely people from 'the rock' we welcomed as our own
They left their homes at lovely Gib, their safety to maintain
And until the war was over, Broughshane would be their home

The camps they were the best, we had to make them feel at home
So Drumack was well modified with school and church as well
They gave no trouble, old or young and settled down at once
The lush green meadows round the camps where wildlife did abound
The singing birds at springtime was very new to some
And the River Braid flowed past the camp and swimming
                                                    could be done

Across the road, Alex's Farms, and the famous Echo Hill
And in wintertime when ice was here, it was the place to go
Alex taught them how to skate and enjoy the winter sport
The sloping braes of Echo Hill, I think they won't forget
Echo Hill was also known as Patterson's on the map

There were some girls of beauty and one was very special,
Sylvia Savarinau her name
And this young beauty took his heart and a friendship did begin
One night he nearly lost her while walking on the road
A car came round the corner and hit her as it passed
But God was very good to her and her young life was saved

Young men came from all around, these lovely girls to see
And some of them got married and in Ulster did remain
The families they have grown up, three generations now
By the time it did come round to go back to their homes again
And Alex, like so many more, their hearts were nearly broke
And the beauty of these lovely girls would linger many years

There is something else that binds us, and it will not go away
It is because we're British and this we will maintain
The British Crown we both uphold
And Elizabeth our Queen
Please God he will maintain our states of Ulster and 'the rock'
God save the Queen!

Patrick McCrory

BABY SAM

You came in the morning with a little quiet cry,
As though you didn't want to wake the world outside.
Didn't you know how long we'd waited for you to arrive?

I held you in the corridor and sang you nursery rhymes.
You felt so small and warm and silent it made me cry . . .
The world rushed on around us. It passed us by.

They weighed you in a bucket and checked you up and down.
They wrote you up in several charts and let me stand around
Wondering if there was a test for miracles they should have done.

And now you'll be the witness of horizons, suns and moons
Of kings and ministers and mysteries, of rainbows and buffoons
And of our love and hopes and dreams over which you'll rule.

You're our one and only Sam in a wide and noisy place,
Where everyone is on the run - it's called the human race.
And you will carry on what years of men have done.
I hope you'll do it better than most of us, my son.

I hope you'll carry with you that ready, radiant smile
With which you greet your family whenever they're close by.
I hope that you'll stay peaceful along life's rolling miles,
As now you sleep so still and sweet in the watches of the night.

But most of all I want you to feel free and open wide
To all that's great and glorious in this crazy patchwork life -
To smell the wind and touch the grass and paint the golden sun,
And catch the elusive fluting of an eternal, dancing song,
A song which plays through all of us, through every race and throng,
Which summons in us harmony and truth and the finest we can give
To make this world a better place in which we all can live.

Big words and thoughts these are for my little baby Sam -
And they'll be bigger still when you become a man.
Meanwhile, you'll see such magic and wonder how it's made . . .
As I confess I wonder at your tiny, smiling face.

Jamie Thomson

FIRST LOVE

Your first love is the sweetest thing
that you will never forget,
no matter how many years pass by
the memories get better yet.
Your heart was awakened to something new
a feeling all cosy and warm,
it made you feel all queasy inside
but at the same time your emotions were torn.
You had only ever known to love
your parents and siblings too,
yet there you are with similar feelings
but with an extra special boost.
This added 'extra' was a sexual thing
that's as natural as can be,
cos when we are attracted to the opposite sex
it's just nature's way you see.
But like everything else you experience first
it goes down in your mind's history book,
so as we get older and the years pass us by
we can close our eyes for another look.

Kriss Simone

HE GAVE ME LIFE

He breathed life back into me
When all I wanted to do was die
He lavished me with beautiful love and affection
When I had not experienced the beautiful love, intimacy and
                                        warmth of a man for years
He brought sunshine and beautiful blue skies
Into my icy, windswept and overcast world
When all I had known was turmoil and sadness
He satisfied my desires, reassured me in times of doubt.
He restored my confidence and gave me the strength to
                                        challenge the world.
He taught me that life was too precious to give up
He gave me reason to carry on living, by becoming a loyal companion
In a fickle and promiscuous world he made me a new woman
By loving me and giving me life.

Ann Grimwood

THE KEY

We gave her the key to the door,
We gave her a 21st key.
The key to unlock not only a door,
But the key to unlock her heart.

It was the key to unlock the door to all secrets,
Or to keep them locked away forever.
The key to share with her loving beau,
As they unlock their lives together.

The key to all true friendships,
The key to all true love.
The key to a golden future,
To a love which will never end.

Janet Cavill

BREAD PUDDING DAY

Three-thirty exact, the lesson bell jangled
'cross my shoulder, half-open
my old satchel dangled
grabbing my coat, out I had rushed
foregoing the after-school match
it's Tuesday today
my treat awaited on Gran's baking tray

as I hastened thru' the open back door
the spicy aroma pervaded the kitchen air
already prepared was my weekly share
over there on the grate
piping hot on the plate
golden brown sugar, sprinkled honey
bread pudding, moreish and yummy

moist, mouth-watering confection
succulent sultana-filled delectation
shredded suet, stale bread soaked overnight
large egg newly laid
in Gran's hands lovingly made
home-baked, cooked special
for her favourite young grandson

Brian Strand

SURPRISE PARTY

I must be the first to tell you,
I've been dying to all week,
The suspense has been killing me,
The surprise we hope a treat,
We've rushed about all weekdays,
Deciding what to do,
Then we thought a party was the
Nicest thing for you.

The caterers are lousy,
But they'll do just for this day,
For they're the only people,
We could get and yet not pay,
The party guests you'll know them,
All friends of yours we hope,
They kept the secret rather well,
But then they promised not to tell,
Well now this rhyme is over,
I think I speak for all,
Best wishes on your birthday,
And many, many more.

Janet Evans

GLASS

I thought you spoke my name
It was as if you were here today
As though it could be the same
When you're away

Leaves flutter and fall
Their shadows dance on the wall
The scion's standing tall
And you're away

The picture, through the glass
Remains, as lovers pass
To show me some things last
When you're away

He's here because he wants her
She makes him wish he'd want to stay
I watch it from my window
And you're away

I know your shadow well;
Fleeting and fragile, vague and fey
It faded as it fell and you're away

The photograph is changed
The scenery is the same
The torch is still aflame
And you're away, you're away . . .

Gayna Florence Perry

GEMMA

a precious gem
at the moment of her birth
i thanked God for this
precious gift
dark hair big hazel eyes
that gazed trustingly
into mine
the years passed so quickly
and now my child is a woman
a beautiful kind-hearted soul
i know one day her heart she will
give to another
as destiny declares
my heart will be glad
but also silently weep
for my baby
my life's gem
the ache in my heart will
stay forever empty
my love for her will continue
relentless
my daughter Gemma

Wendy-Elizabeth Smith

A GAZE HELD BETWEEN US

Embedded between daffodils your eyes stand bold.
A pair of sparkling sapphires I find.
Sailing into a blue beauty, eyes so calm,
Across layers of water, I'm safe.
Dive into your pools of thought
Through shades of blue,
They care and cradle me
As I swim within your eyes.
Within those eyes I trust,
They hold my darkest secrets.
And they hold my gaze,
I'm sealed within blue envelopes
And you relieve the anxiety from my eyes.

Weaved the thick daffodils wearing four cotton socks,
A chocolate-dipped face became visible,
With your clotted cream chest and caramel back
And your elegant tail of flowing fur.

But the blueness in your eyes stays forever in my mind,
They are planted there like forget-me-nots.
You cast the rainbow over my world.
But the arch of blue, the colour that does not fade,
Stands forever and shines within me.
Through your eyes I see a world
That reflects the smiles of the sun.
Inside the pot of gold there is no gold,
A pair of sparkling sapphires I find.
I found the eyes that give me happiness.
And blueness in your eyes will be forever in my eyes,
Forever in my mind
There they bloom forever, beautiful forget-me-nots.

Kathryn Diane West

FROM CHILDHOOD MEMORIES (OF BRIXHAM, DEVON)

When the fair came to Brixham
When they had their regatta,
The huge traction engines
Kicked up such a clatter.
They rumbled down Fore Street,
Went round by the quay,
A sight that the visitors
Came there to see.
They thought they'd not make it
Up Overgang hill,
To their place on the green
They puffed on with a will.
I remember the side-shows,
The steam carousel,
The people who came
With such goodies to sell.
The big blocks of nougat
A real fairground sweet,
With nuts, fruit and cherries
To us such a treat.
I recall with great pleasure
The firework display
That always took place
At the end of their stay.
And those three days of fun
I shall never forget,
Those memories of childhood
Forever green yet.

Margaret B Baguley

WELL-REMEMBERED SPECIAL MOMENTS

Some things one never forgets, however old one grows.
In fact, some things seem to become fresher and fresher
My childhood was lovely, out there in the country,
We lived in a cottage with no running water,
No electric, no gas, and a mile away from any shops.

But very special times we often had, and one I always treasure,
We would sit around, some of us on Dad's knee,
To listen to him sing.
He was not a professional singer, but to me it was oh! so good,
As he sang of the old organist in the old village church,

It went like this:
'The preacher in the village church, one Sunday morning said,
'Our organist is ill today, will someone play instead,'
An old man staggered down the aisle, his clothes were old and torn,
But when he touched the organ keys, the melody that followed was,
The sweetest ever heard, and so on, and so on'.

Another song he sang was about the clock that stopped short,
Never to go again when the old man died.

Oh! I look back on those lovely times, and special moments,
And thank God for the wonderful happy years of my childhood,
And for a Godly mother and a loving caring father.

R Baker

SPECIAL MOMENT

You may remember little things,
Like walking in the park,
Listening to your grandchildren,
Sounds from the singing lark.

These times are all so special,
The fun, the laughter too,
They will make you smile
Then you'll talk awhile
These things make dreams come true.

Think just for one moment,
Whenever you feel down,
I'm sure there will be happy thoughts,
To move away that frown.

All these gifts so special,
Sent from up above,
Surely it's not too much to ask,
A prayer to God is love.

C A Elsmore

SPECIAL MOMENTS

Everyone in their life has a moment,
A moment where time stands still,
A moment where there's just you,

And it's beautiful

And peaceful

And you want it to last forever.

I had that moment,
That *special* moment,
With our two sons - one newborn, one two years old,
When I sat and cradled a child in each arm,

And it was oh so beautiful

And peaceful.

Then my husband came in and looked and smiled,
A simple smile that shone from his heart.

That was *my* moment,

My special moment.

Maxine Williams

SUBMISSIONS INVITED
SOMETHING FOR EVERYONE

POETRY NOW 2003 - Any subject,
any style, any time.

WOMENSWORDS 2003 - Strictly women,
have your say the female way!

STRONGWORDS 2003 - Warning!
Opinionated and have strong views.
(Not for the faint-hearted)

All poems no longer than 30 lines.
Always welcome! No fee!
Cash Prizes to be won!

Mark your envelope (eg *Poetry Now) 2003*
Send to:
Forward Press Ltd
Remus House, Coltsfoot Drive,
Peterborough, PE2 9JX

**OVER £10,000 POETRY PRIZES
TO BE WON!**

Judging will take place in October 2003